© **Copyright** _____ **2020 - All rights reserved.**

The content contained within this book may not be reproduced, duplicated or transmitted without direct written permission from the author or the publisher.

Under no circumstances will any blame or legal responsibility be held against the publisher, or author, for any damages, reparation, or monetary loss due to the information contained within this book. Either directly or indirectly. You are responsible for your own choices, actions, and results.

Legal Notice:

This book is copyright protected. This book is only for personal use. You cannot amend, distribute, sell, use, quote or paraphrase any part, or the content within this book, without the consent of the author or publisher.

Disclaimer Notice:

Please note the information contained within this document is for educational and entertainment purposes only. All effort has been executed to present accurate, up to date, and reliable, complete information. No warranties of any kind are declared or implied. Readers acknowledge that the author is not engaging in the rendering of legal, financial, medical or professional advice. The content within this book has been derived from various sources. Please consult a licensed professional before attempting any techniques outlined in this book.

By reading this document, the reader agrees that under no circumstances is the author responsible for any losses, direct or indirect, which are incurred as a result of the use of the information contained within this document, including, but not limited to, — errors, omissions, or inaccuracies.

HELLO AND WELCOME

TRAINS ARE FUN AND EXCITING AND IN THIS TRAIN ACTIVITY BOOK YOU WILL BE ABLE TO DRAW, FIND, SEARCH AND COLOR MANY TRAIN THEMED ACTIVITIES INCLUDING STORY BASED MAZES- CHECK OUT OUR BACK PAGE FOR EXAMPLES

GRAB SOME COLOUR PENCILS, A PEN, PENCIL AND BE EXCITED TO COMPLETE THIS ACTIVITY BOOK.

ACTIVITIES INCLUDE
- STORY MAZES
- COLORING PAGES
- WORD SEARCH
- DESIGN YOUR OWN
- SPOT THE DIFFERENCE
- MATH WORKSHEETS
- WORD SCRAMBLE
- AND MORE

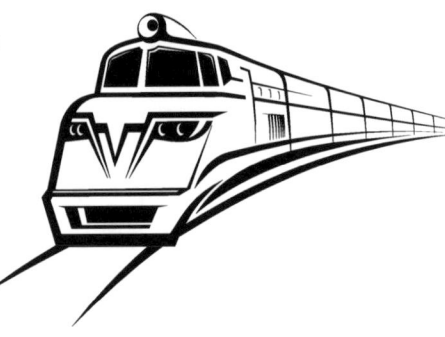

THIS BOOK BELONGS TO

_____

CAN YOU COMPLETE THE TRAIN DOT TO DOT?

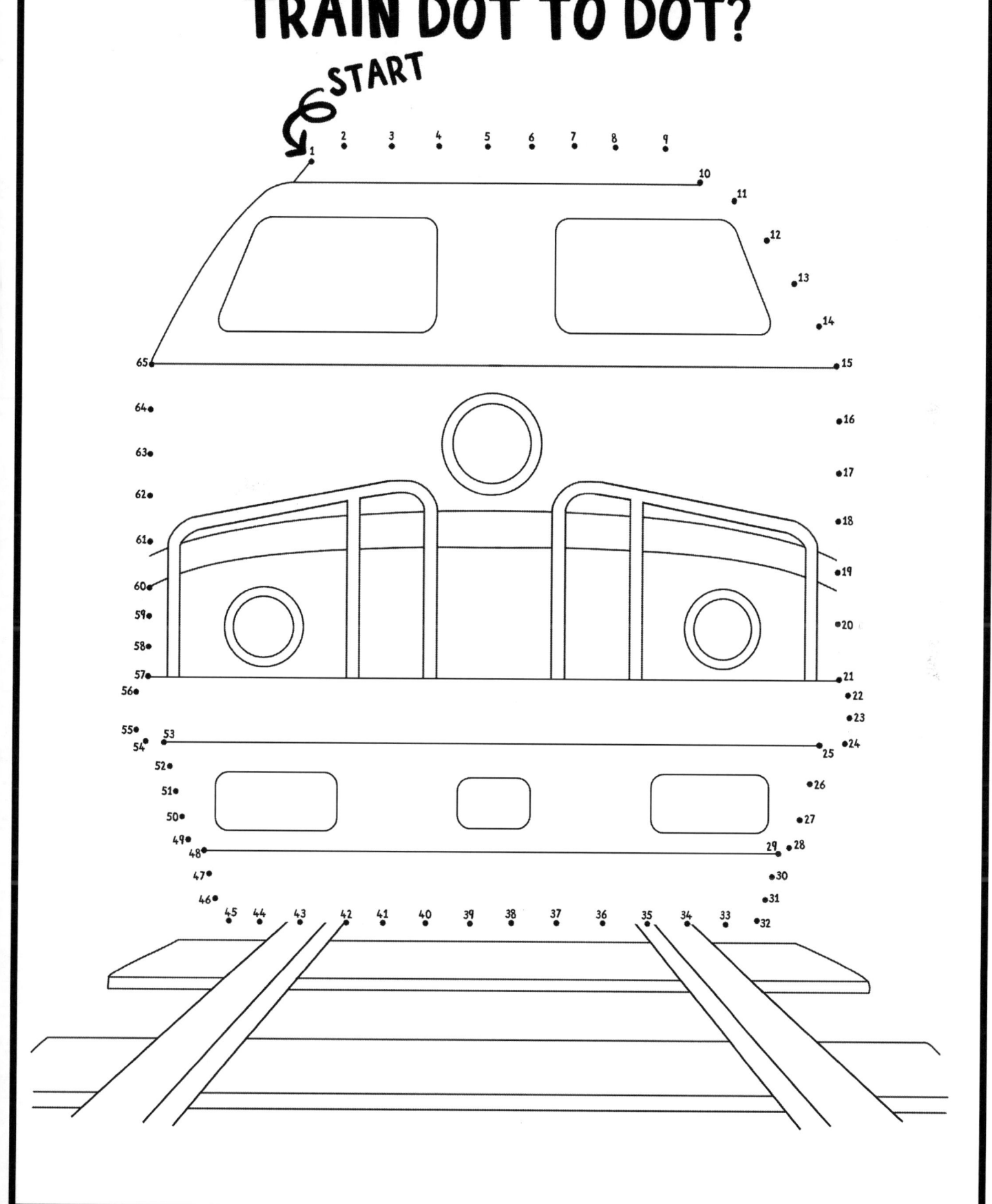

CAN YOU COMPLETE THE TRAIN MAZE?

LETS COUNT THE TRAINS
USE THE PICTURES THAT EQUAL TO THE NUMBERS TO SOLVE THE EQUATIONS

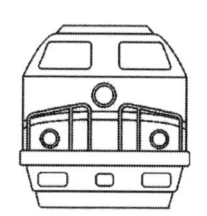

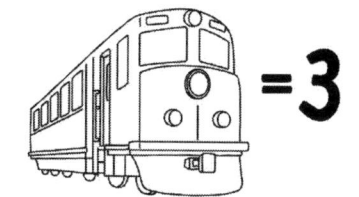

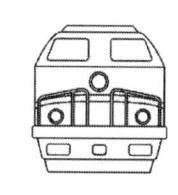

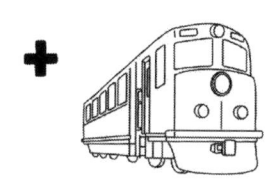

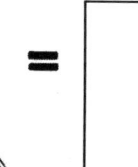

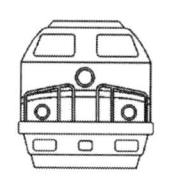

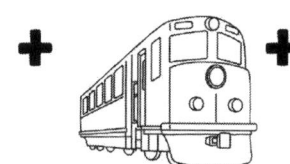

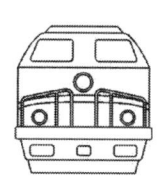

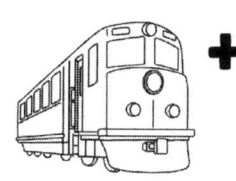

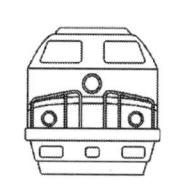

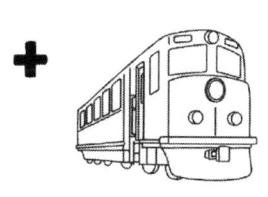

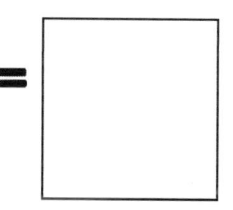

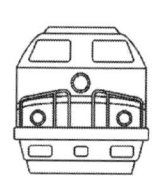

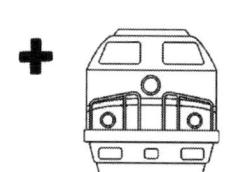

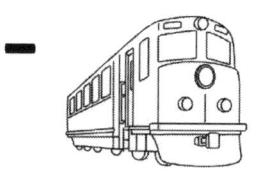

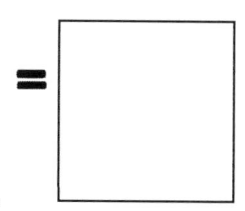

🚂 =1   🚆 =2   🚄 =3

🚂 + 🚆 + 🚄 + 🚂 = ☐

🚆 + 🚄 + 🚆 + 🚂 = ☐

🚄 + 🚆 + 🚄 − 🚂 = ☐

🚆 + 🚆 − 🚄 − 🚂 = ☐

ASK A GROWN UP TO HELP

CAN YOU FIND THE ITEMS IN THE PICTURE BELOW?

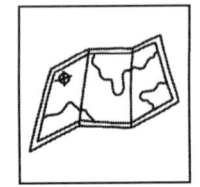

CAN YOU DESIGN YOUR OWN TRAIN ON THE TRACKS?

CAN YOU HELP THE TRAIN GET DOWN THE MOUNTAIN MAZE?

COLOR TIME

CAN YOU HELP THE TRAIN GET TO THE STATION?

CHOOSE THE CORRECT PATH

COLOR THE TRAIN STATION

MATCH THE SHAPES

TRACE THE WORDS ABOUT TRAINS

TRAIN
TICKET
HORN 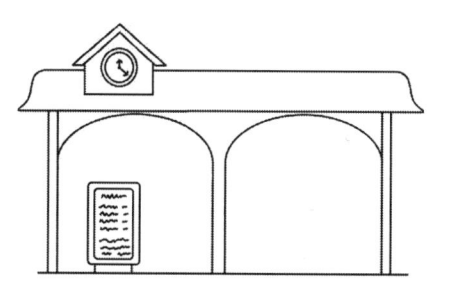
TRACKS 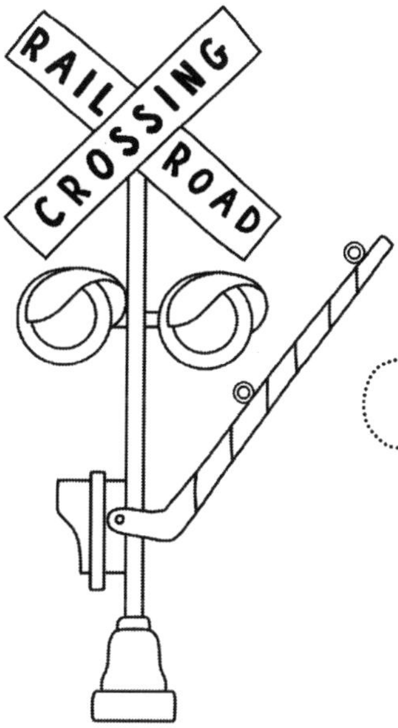
CROSSING 
WHISTLE
STOP
TUNNEL  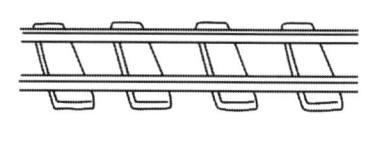
STATION
BRIDGE

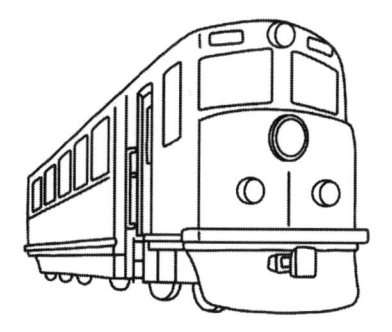

CAN YOU COUNT FROM 1 - 20?
FILL IN THE BOXES WITH THE CORRECT NUMBER

1   ☐   ☐   4   5

6   ☐   8   9   ☐

11   12   ☐   14   15

☐   17   18   19   ☐

FINISH

CAN YOU FIND THE ITEMS IN THE PICTURE BELOW?

COLOR IN THE TRAIN

CAN YOU HELP THE TRAIN GET THROUGH THE TUNNEL MAZE?

COMPLETE THE WORD SEARCH

FIND THESE WORDS
PASSENGER
DEPART
ARRIVE
LUGGAGE
TICKET
TRAVEL

K P X I G T F V B P
C T A Q J A M E T A
A R L B O A V W I S
R A J U H T Q U C S
R V N Y G M W N K E
I E X M I G P V E N
V L O P B M A J T G
E O Z A W R H G I E
V J D E P A R T E R
O M B I J D T W N M

LETS COUNT THE TRAINS ITEMS
USE THE PICTURES THAT EQUAL TO THE NUMBERS TO SOLVE THE EQUATIONS

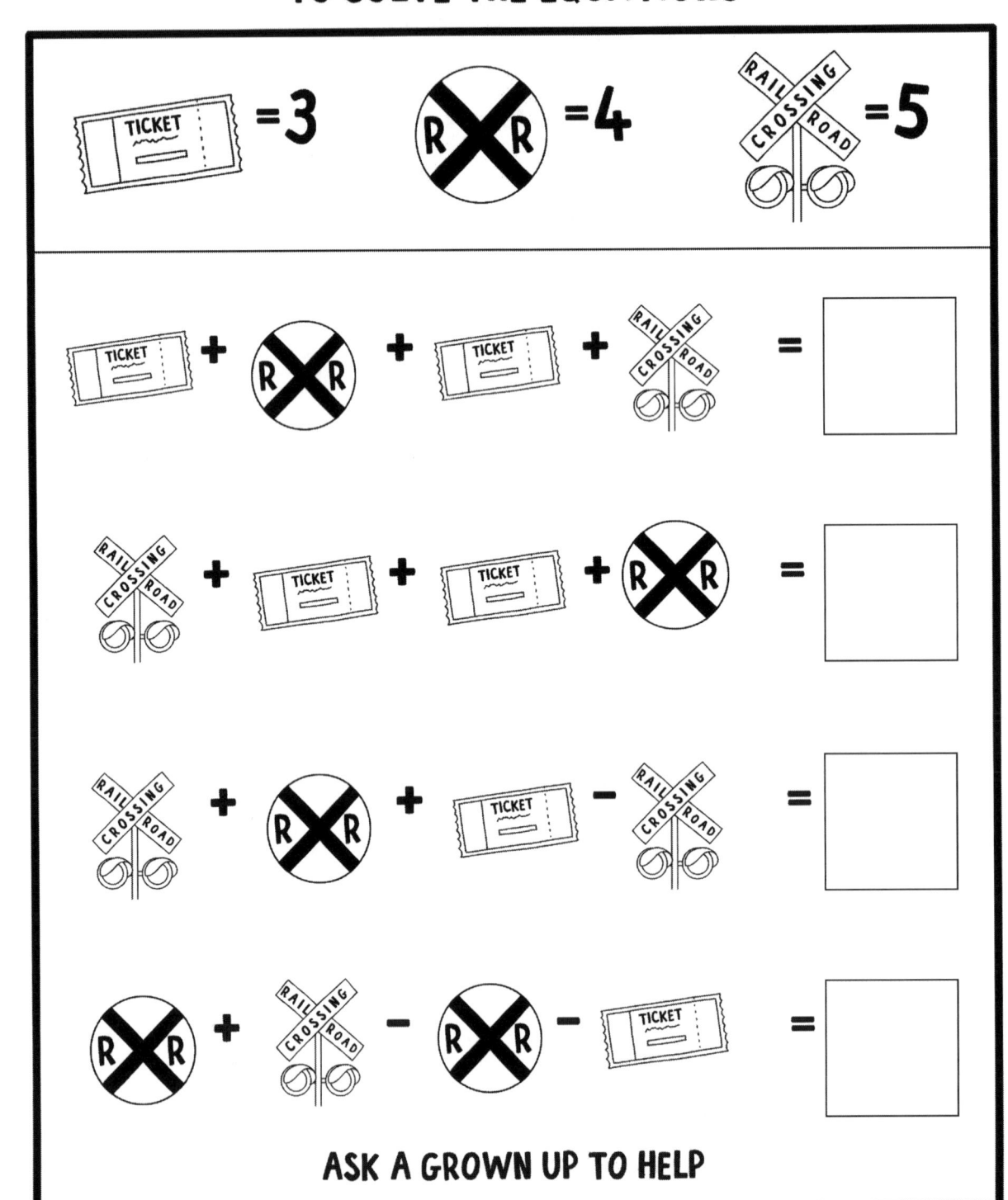

TICKET = 3   RR = 4   RAIL CROSSING = 5

TICKET + RR + TICKET + RAIL CROSSING = ☐

RAIL CROSSING + TICKET + TICKET + RR = ☐

RAIL CROSSING + RR + TICKET − RAIL CROSSING = ☐

RR + RAIL CROSSING − RR − TICKET = ☐

ASK A GROWN UP TO HELP

COMPLETE THE IMAGE OF THE TRAIN CART
COLOR IN

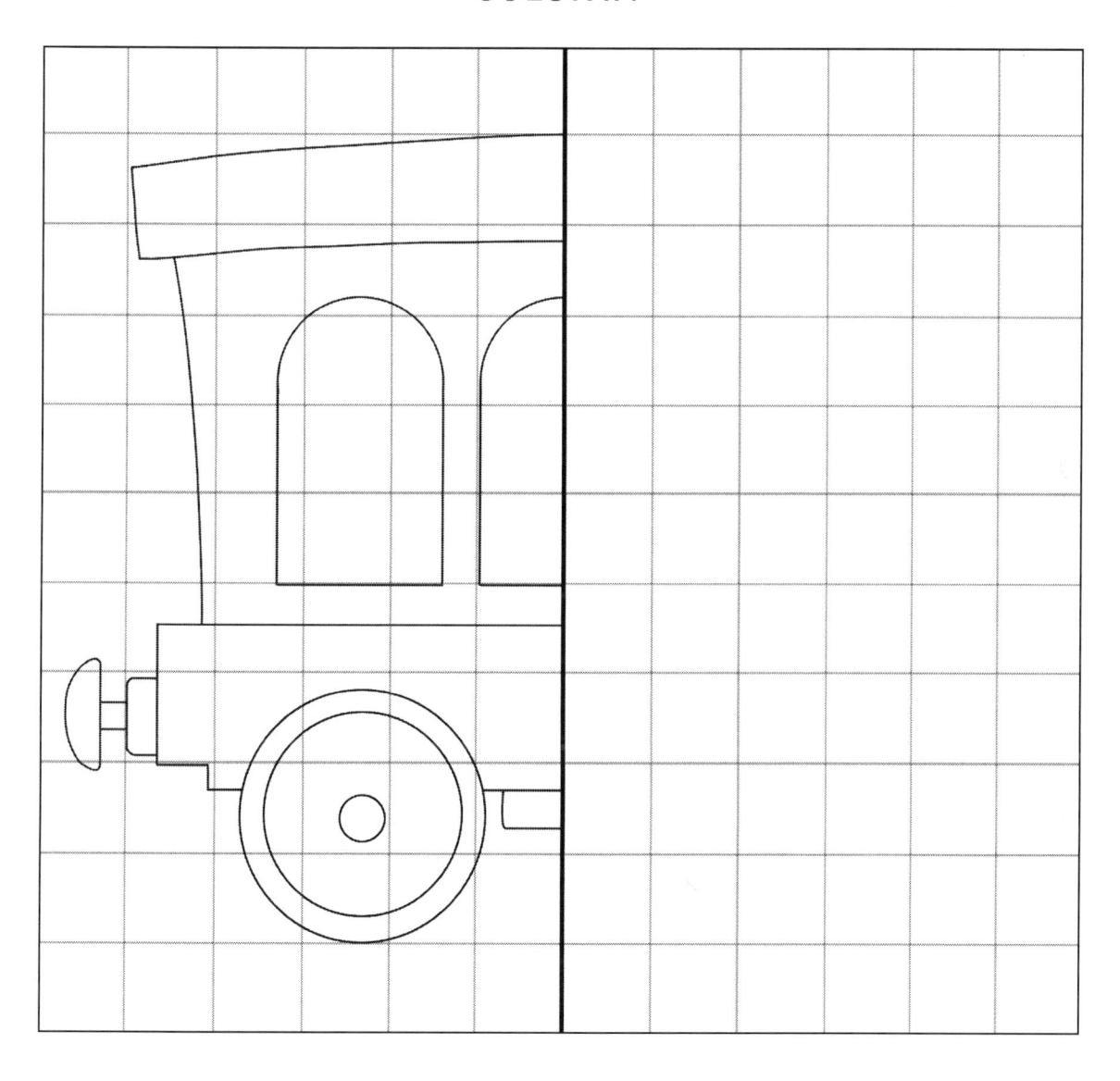

HINT

COLOR IN THE TRAIN

TRAINS ARE COOL

CAN YOU COMPLETE THE TRAIN SIGN MAZE?

START

CAN YOU COUNT HOW MANY?

COLOR TIME

CAN YOU SPOT THE 4 DIFFERENCES?
CIRCLE THE DIFFERENCES BELOW

COMPLETE THE WORD SEARCH

FIND THESE WORDS
CABOOSE
CARGO
BOXCAR
FREIGHT
LOCOMOTIVE
TRAIN

O F V G T O K O D L
V J O T R W Q Q Z O
T I I R A V V H L C
C Y Q L I Q T C I O
A N V O N L Q V B M
R C A B O O S E O O
G Y X B S R C Q X T
O L L L O M C L C I
N A I L U D F U A V
F R E I G H T M R E

CAN YOU COMPLETE THE TRAIN MAZE?

START

WHICH LETTER WILL HELP YOU FINISH THE TRAIN MAZE?

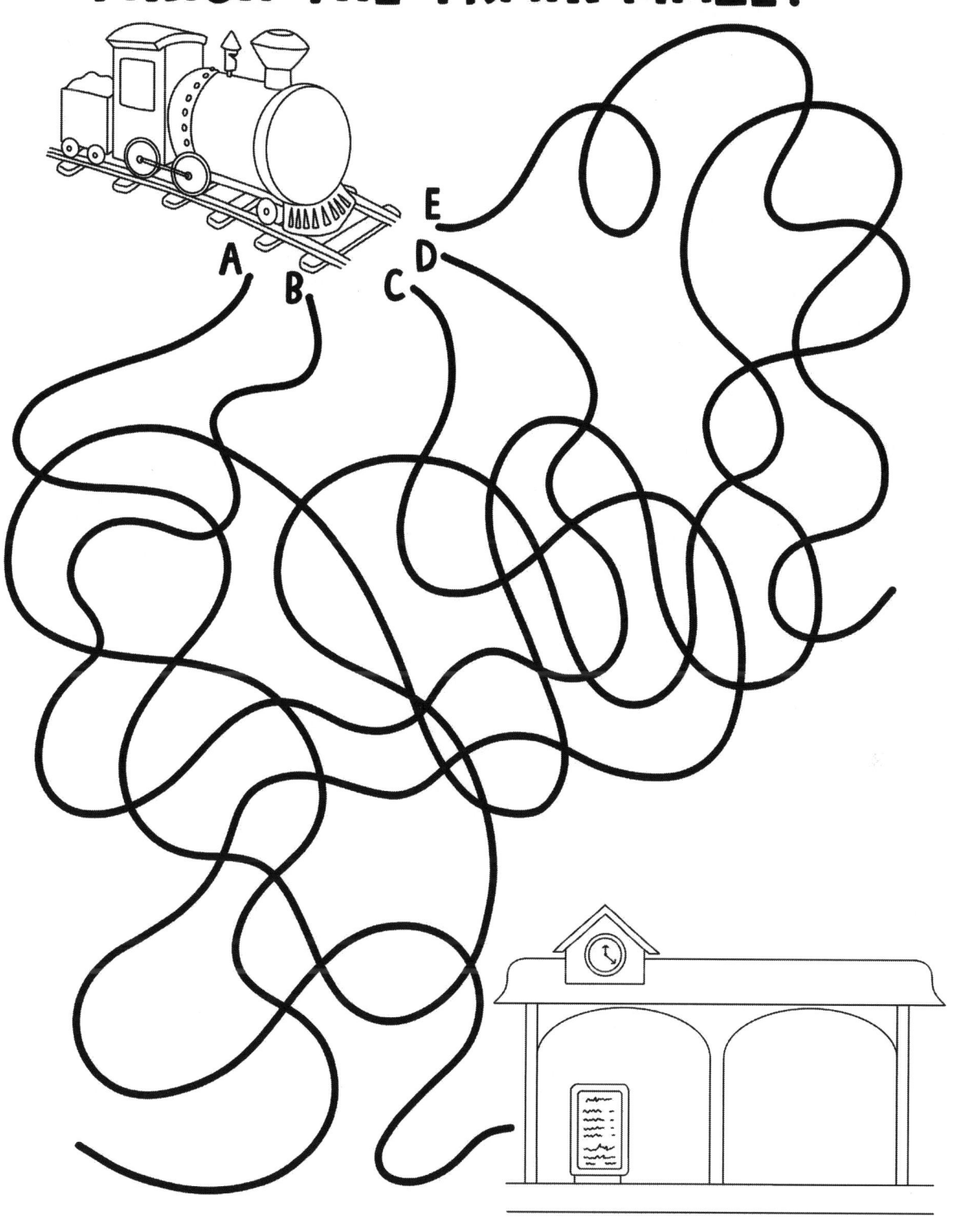

COLOR IN THE GOODS TRAIN

TRAINS CAN ALSO BE SLOW

COMPLETE THE IMAGE OF THE TRAIN CART
COLOR IN

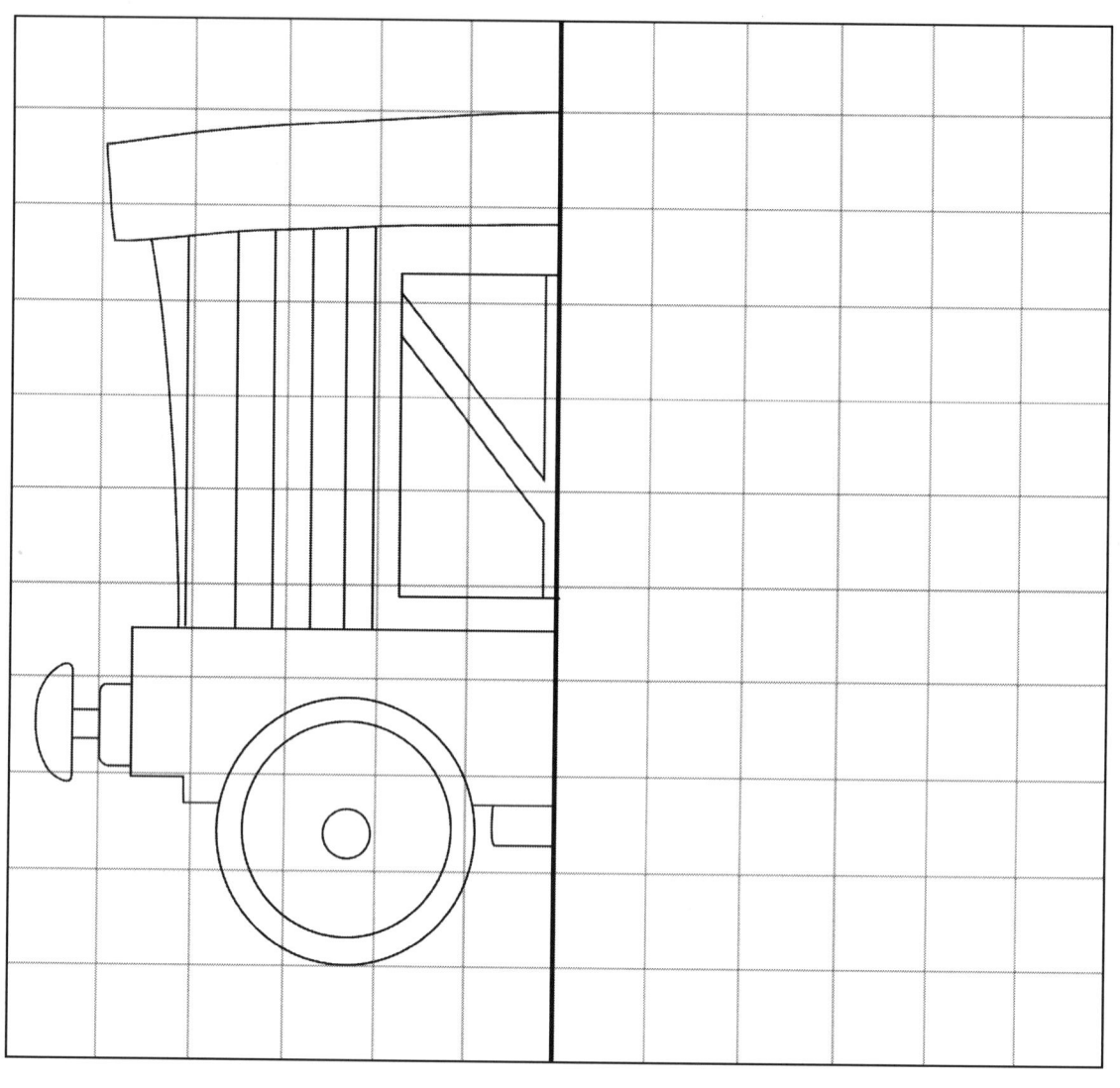

HINT

CAN YOU COMPLETE THE CONDUCTOR HAT MAZE?

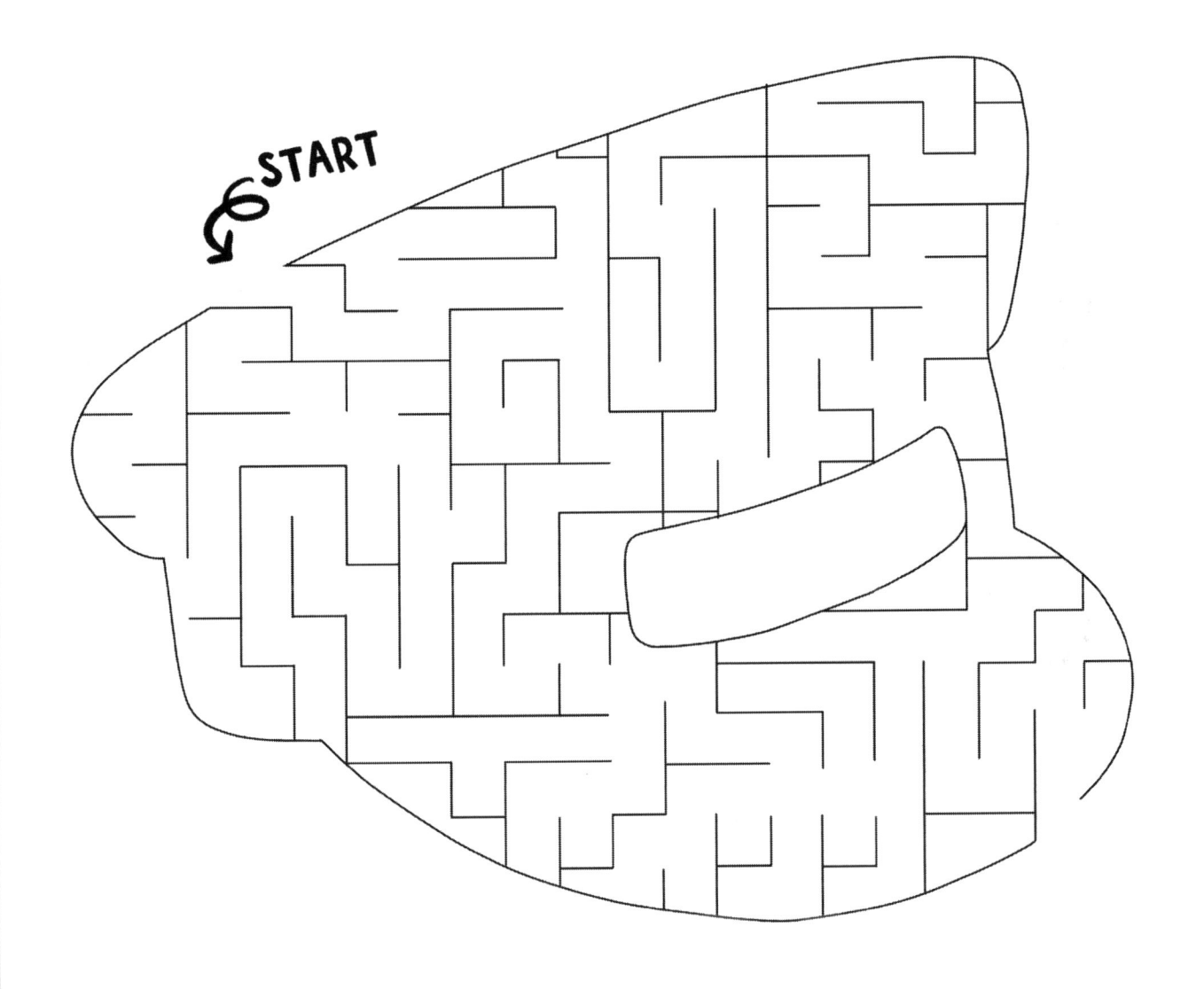

START

COMPLETE THE WORD SEARCH

FIND THESE WORDS

TUNNEL
BRIDGE
STATION
TRACKS
RAILS
RAILROAD

```
B R I D G E R T Y Q
J R K T Y P E R A P
I A G U K O H A L T
W I D G E S A C J U
O L I S V L F K H N
D R D K E I R S X N
Q O U V Q T A L V E
T A S T A T I O N L
I D Y M Q Q L X X L
O N A O G S S H H Z
```

COLOR IN THE TRAIN

CAN YOU DESIGN YOUR OWN TRAIN ON THE TRACKS?

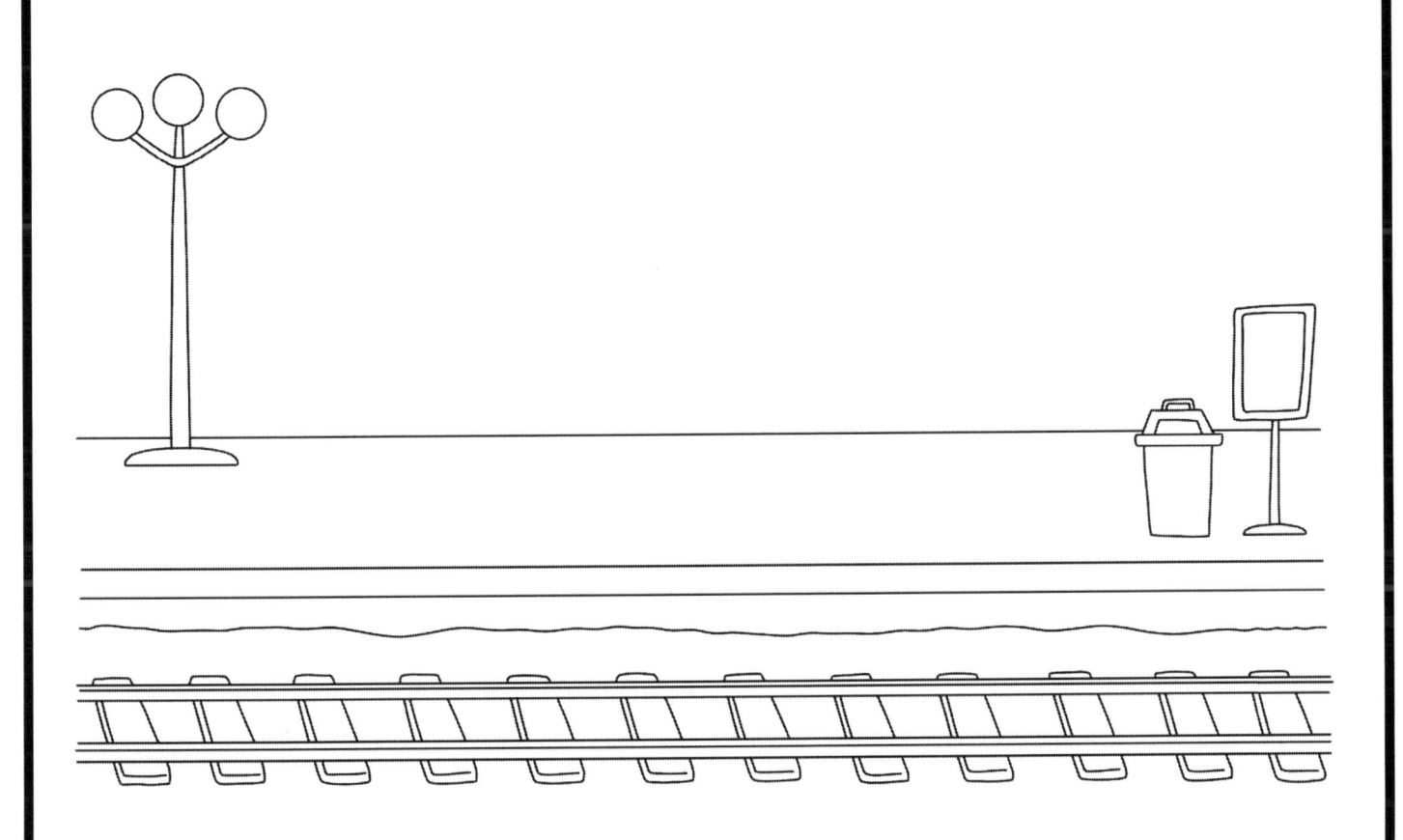

CAN YOU UNSCRAMBLE THESE WORDS?

ASK A GROWN UP FOR HELP

ANTIR _ _ _ _ _

WLEEH _ _ _ _ _

KCART _ _ _ _ _

HNOR _ _ _ _

TKCIET _ _ _ _ _ _

NAOTSTI _ _ _ _ _ _ _

GSNI _ _ _ _

NLETUN _ _ _ _ _ _

COLOR IN THE SIGN

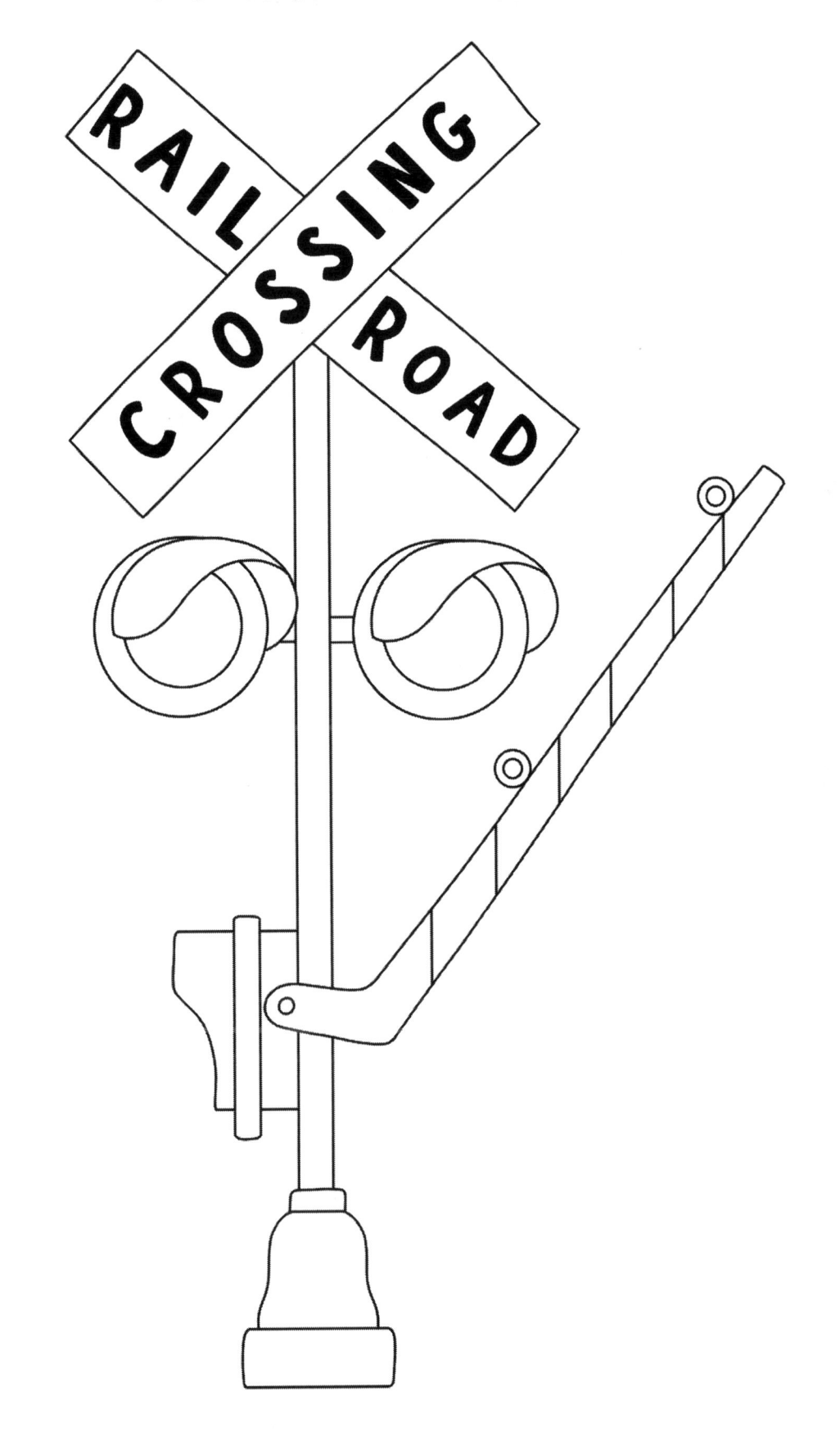

RAIL CROSSING ROAD

CAN YOU FIND THE ODD ONE OUT?

FIND THE WORDS
USE THE PICTURES BELOW OR ASK AN ADULT FOR HELP

```
F W W K B Q C H O W
N P H T J T I F K W
L C E W B Z R K K I
T N E T O T B A M S
L E L R T G W W C G
L T U A R I V M K
S I I J Q C A D X
I Z W N S O I K V V
G T U N N E L G E W
N M G E V L R L E T
```

CAN YOU COUNT HOW MANY?

COLOR IN THE TRAIN

CAN YOU COMPLETE THE TRAIN MAZE?

START

ADDITION AND SUBTRACTION FUN
HOW QUICK CAN YOU SOLVE THESE

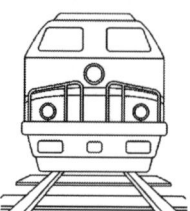

1) 7
   + 2
   ___

2) 9
   − 8
   ___

3) 5
   + 4
   ___

4) 6
   − 1
   ___

5) 3
   + 3
   ___

6) 4
   + 2
   ___

7) 9
   + 2
   ___

8) 7
   − 3
   ___

9) 5
   − 2
   ___

10) 3
    + 2
    ___

11) 6
    + 4
    ___

12) 9
    − 3
    ___

13) 6
    − 3
    ___

14) 7
    + 6
    ___

15) 8
    + 8
    ___

COMPLETE THE IMAGE OF THE RAILROAD CROSSING SIGN
COLOR IN

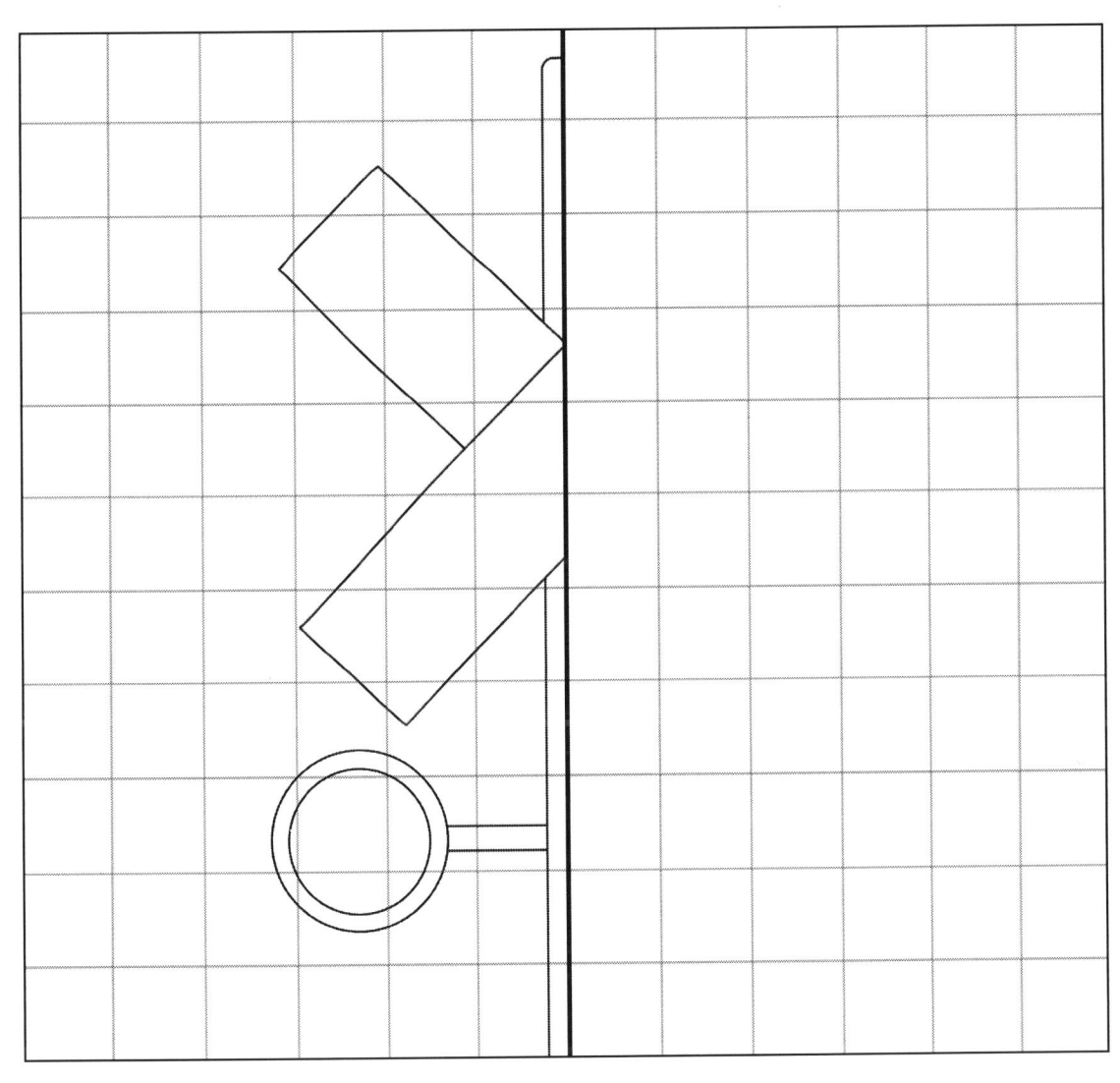

HINT

TRAIN SUDOKU
THIS IS A PICTURE OF TRAIN SUDUKO, PUT EACH ITEM SO THEY APPEAR ONCE IN EACH OF THE BELOW BOXES DRAW THEM IN

ROW COLUMN

CAN YOU COMPLETE THE TRAIN DOT TO DOT?

CAN YOU FIND THE ODD ONE OUT?

COMPLETE THE WORD SEARCH

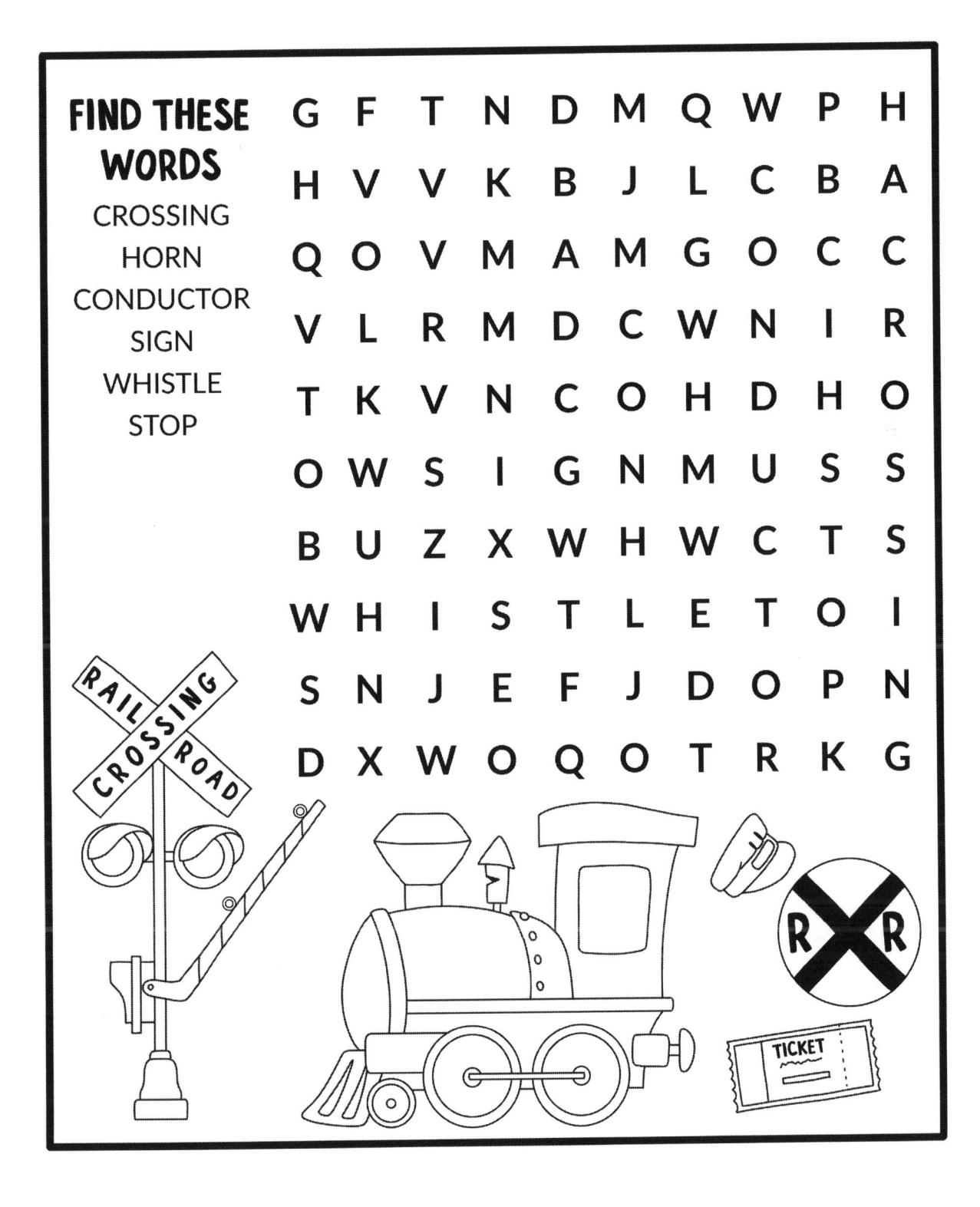

FIND THESE WORDS
- CROSSING
- HORN
- CONDUCTOR
- SIGN
- WHISTLE
- STOP

```
G F T N D M Q W P H
H V V K B J L C B A
Q O V M A M G O C C
V L R M D C W N I R
T K V N C O H D H O
O W S I G N M U S S
B U Z X W H W C T S
W H I S T L E T O I
S N J E F J D O P N
D X W O Q O T R K G
```

CAN YOU COMPLETE THE TRAIN MAZE?

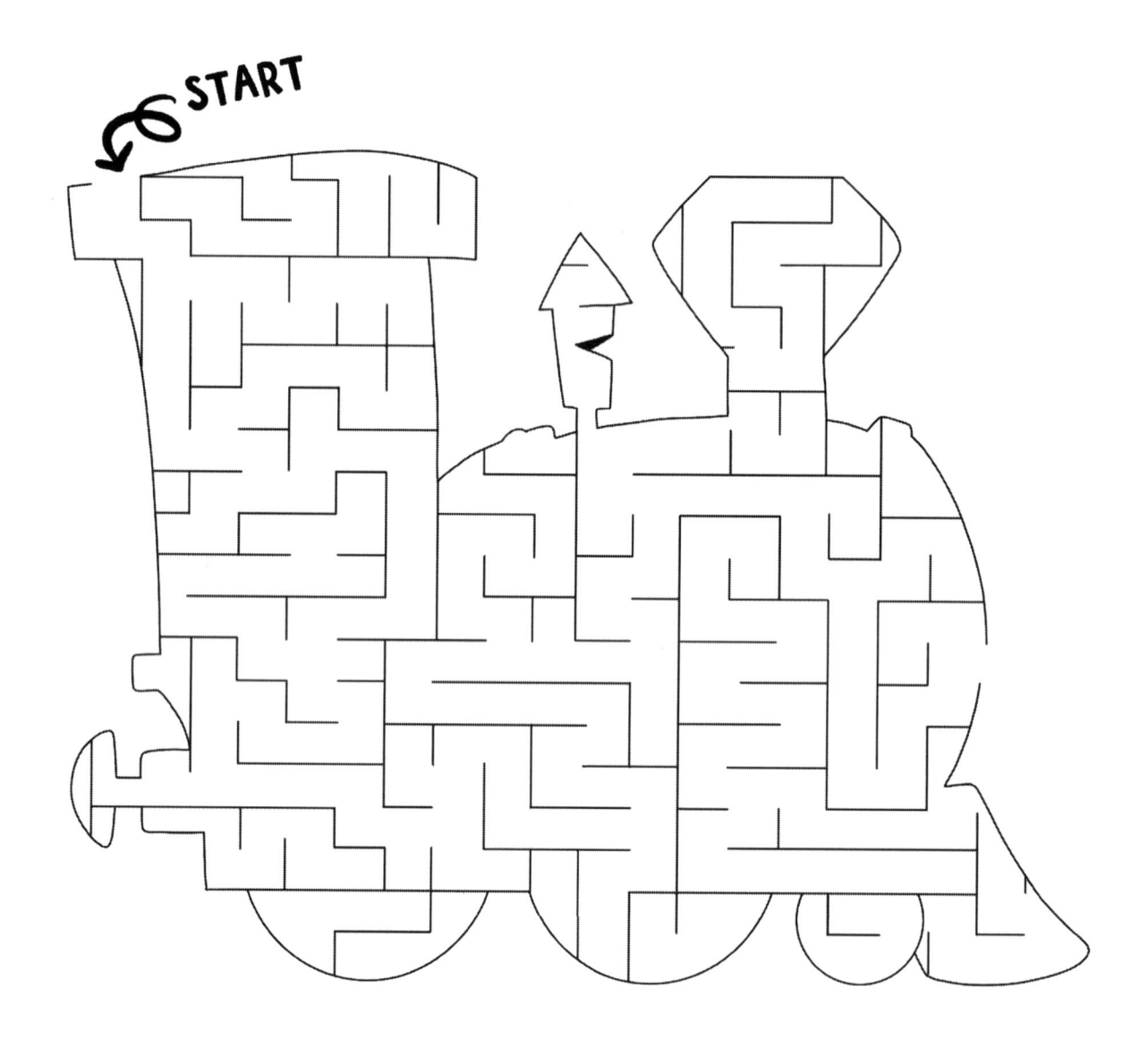

START

COMPLETE THE WORD SEARCH

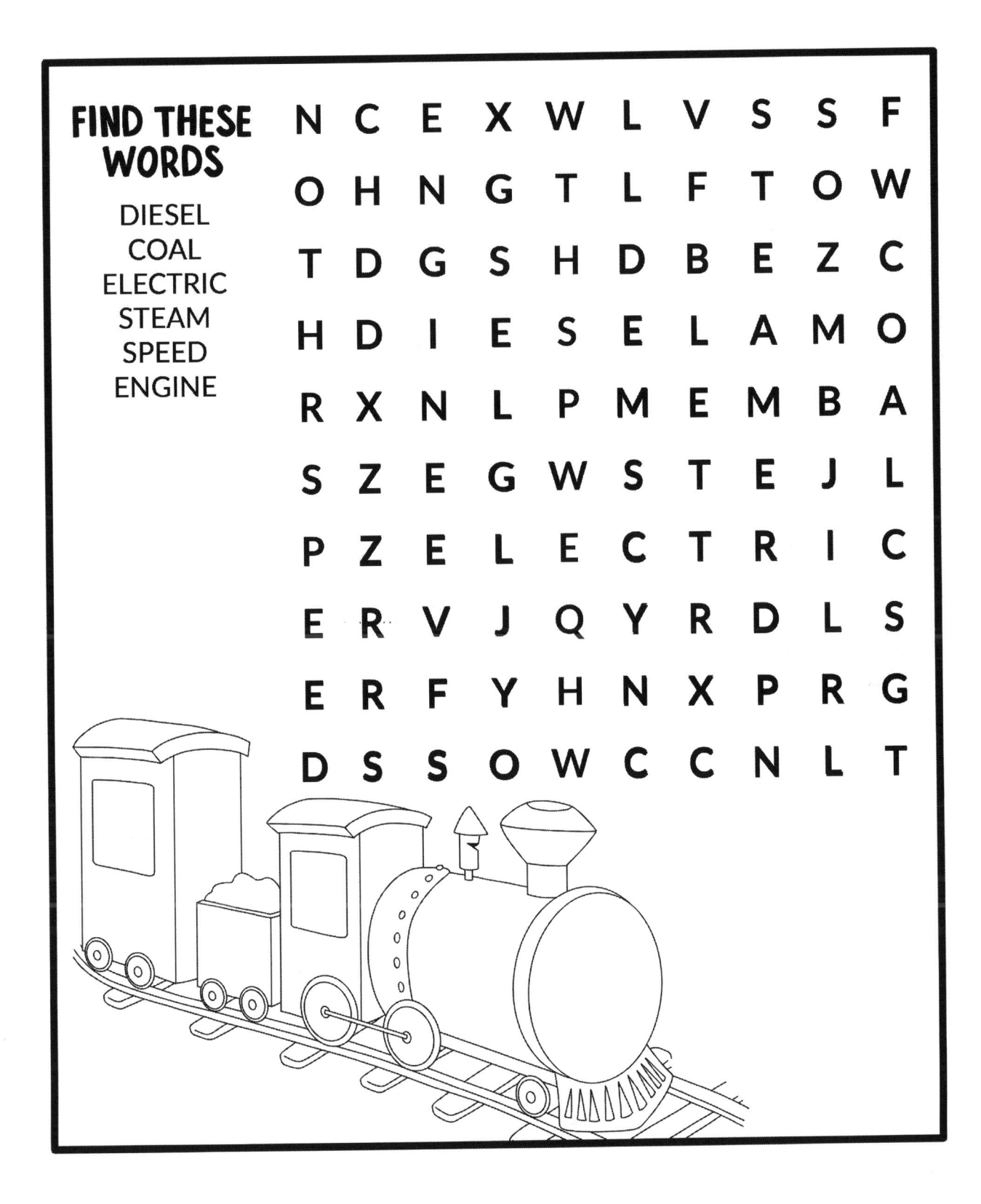

FIND THESE WORDS

- DIESEL
- COAL
- ELECTRIC
- STEAM
- SPEED
- ENGINE

N	C	E	X	W	L	V	S	S	F
O	H	N	G	T	L	F	T	O	W
T	D	G	S	H	D	B	E	Z	C
H	D	I	E	S	E	L	A	M	O
R	X	N	L	P	M	E	M	B	A
S	Z	E	G	W	S	T	E	J	L
P	Z	E	L	E	C	T	R	I	C
E	R	V	J	Q	Y	R	D	L	S
E	R	F	Y	H	N	X	P	R	G
D	S	S	O	W	C	C	N	L	T

COLOR IN THE TRAIN

CAN YOU SPOT THE 4 DIFFERENCES?
CIRCLE THE DIFFERENCES BELOW

COLOR THE FAST TRAIN

SOLUTIONS IF YOU NEED THEM

ANSWER KEY ODD ONE OUT

ANSWER SPOT THE DIFFERENCE

ANSWER KEY MAZE

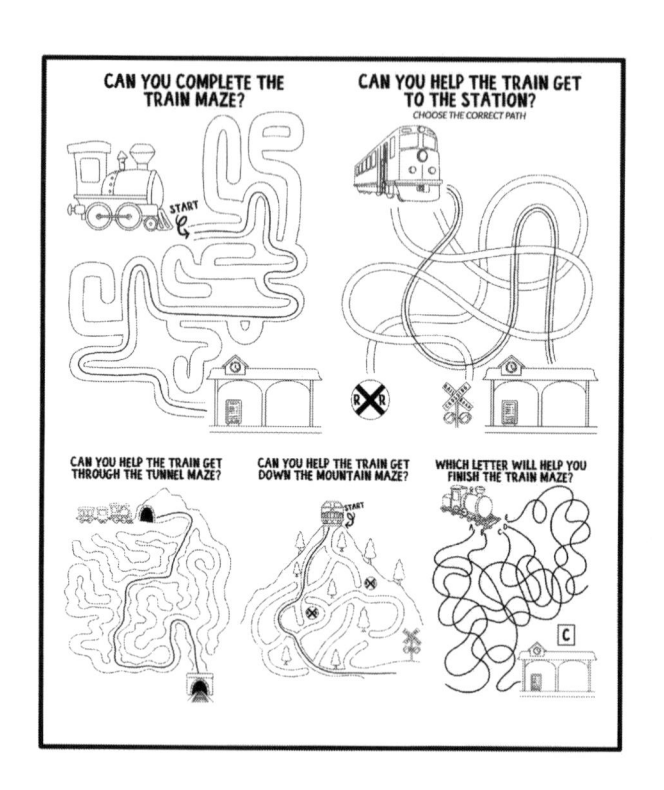

ANSWER KEY MATH

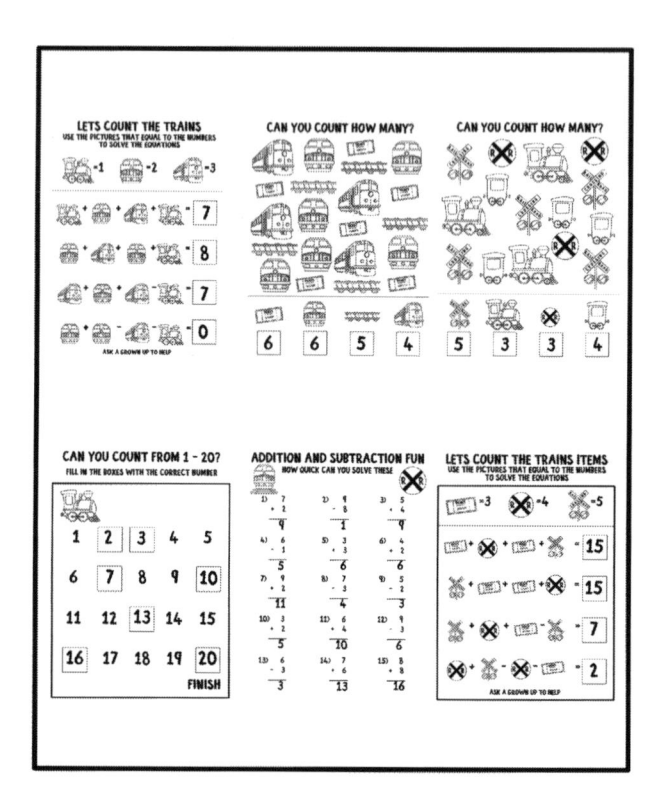

ANSWER KEY TRAIN SUDOKU

ANSWER KEY FIND THE WORDS

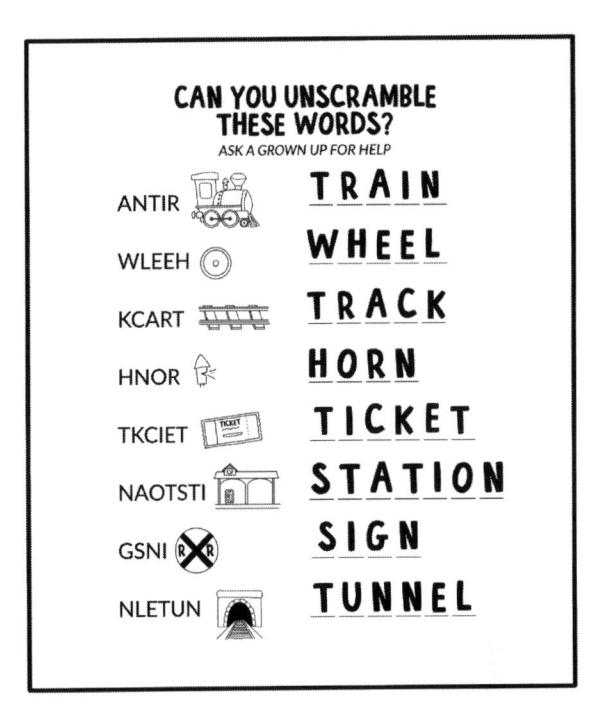

CAN YOU UNSCRAMBLE THESE WORDS?
ASK A GROWN UP FOR HELP

- ANTIR — T R A I N
- WLEEH — W H E E L
- KCART — T R A C K
- HNOR — H O R N
- TKCIET — T I C K E T
- NAOTSTI — S T A T I O N
- GSNI — S I G N
- NLETUN — T U N N E L

ANSWER KEY WORD SEARCH

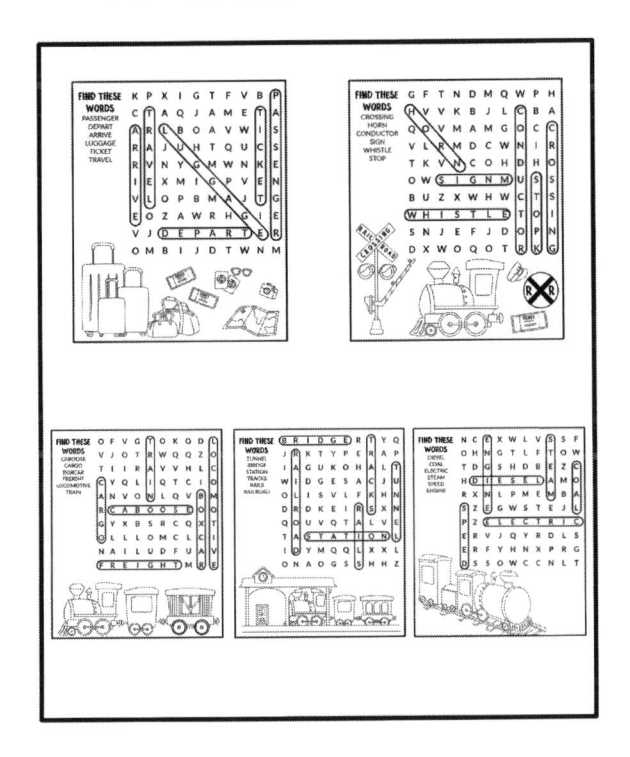

ANSWER KEY MATCH

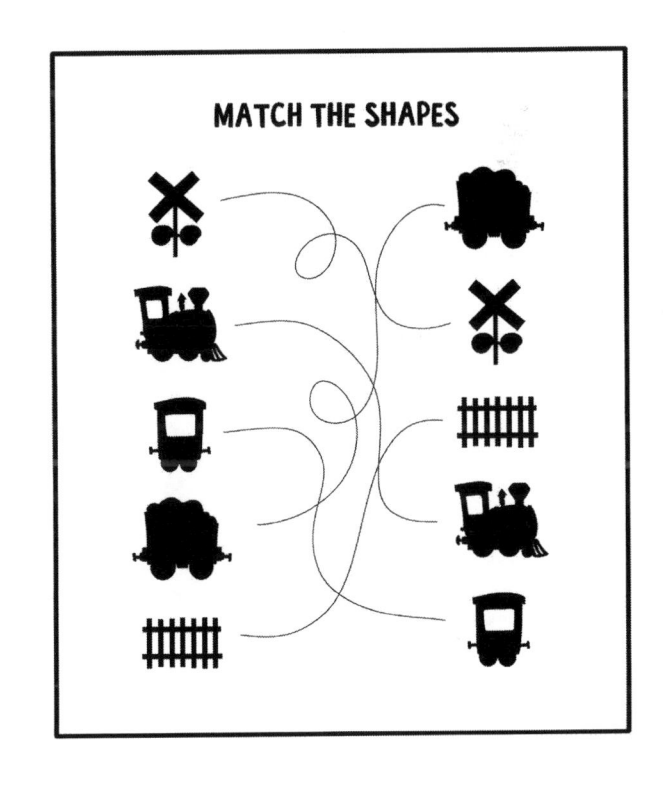

MATCH THE SHAPES

ANSWER KEY FIND THE WORDS

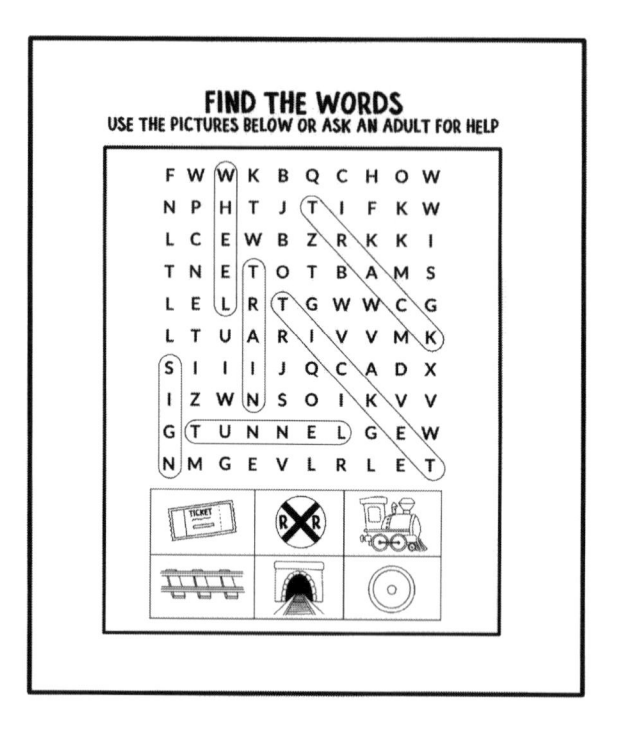

ANSWER KEY ODD ONE OUT

ANSWER KEY SHAPE MAZE

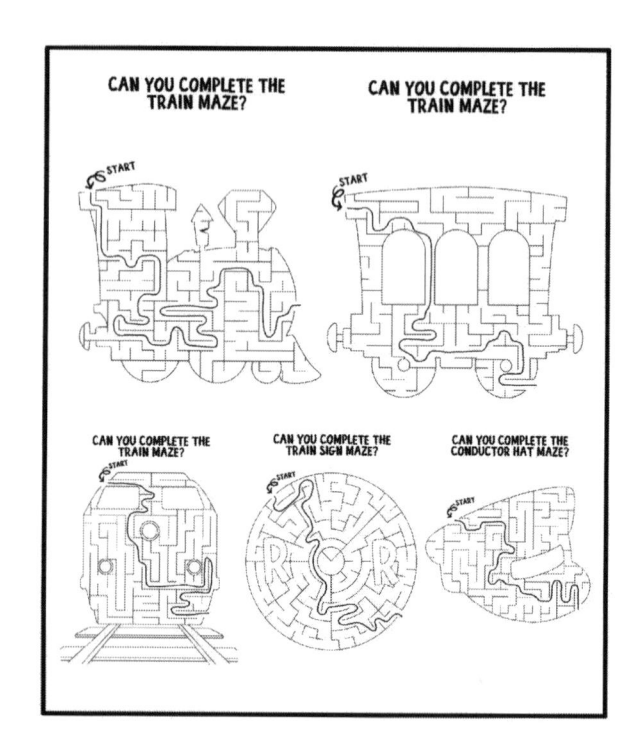

ANSWER KEY ODD ONE OUT